The
Mountain Poems
of Hsieh Ling-yün

OTHER TRANSLATIONS BY DAVID HINTON

Tao Te Ching *(Counterpoint)*

The Selected Poems of Po Chü-i *(New Directions)*

The Analects *(Counterpoint)*

Mencius *(Counterpoint)*

Chuang Tzu: The Inner Chapters *(Counterpoint)*

The Late Poems of Meng Chiao *(Princeton)*

The Selected Poems of Li Po *(New Directions)*

The Selected Poems of T'ao Ch'ien *(Copper Canyon)*

The Selected Poems of Tu Fu *(New Directions)*

The
Mountain Poems
of Hsieh Ling-yün

Translated by
DAVID HINTON

A NEW DIRECTIONS BOOK

ACKNOWLEDGMENTS:

Translation of this book was supported in part by grants from The Charles Engelhard Foundation and The National Endowment for the Humanities.

Manufactured in the United States of America
New Directions Books are published on acid-free paper.
First published as New Directions Paperbook 928 in 2001
Book design by Sylvia Frezzolini Severance
Map by Molly O'Halloran

Library of Congress Cataloging-in-Publication Data

Xie, Lingyun, 385-433.
    [Poems. Selection. English.]
    The mountain poems of Hsieh Ling-yün ; translated by David Hinton.
        p. cm.
    "A new directions book."
    Includes bibliographical references.
    ISBN 0-8112-1489-3

1. Xie, Lingyun, 385-433—Translations into English.   I. Hinton, David, 1954-   II. Title.

PL2666.H75 A24 2001
895,1'124—dc21

                                                            2001030715

New Directions Books are published for James Laughlin
by New Directions Publishing Corporation,
80 Eighth Avenue, New York, NY 10011

CONTENTS

Introduction   vii

Map   xvi

First Exile: Yung-chia 422-23 (C.E.)

On a Tower Beside the Lake   3

Inspecting Farmlands, I Climb the Bay's Coil-Isle Mountain   4

Climbing Green-Cliff Mountain in Yung-chia   5

The Journey Home   6

Mountain Dwelling: Shih-ning 423-432

I've Put in Gardens South of the Fields, Opened Up . . .   9

There Are Towering Peaks on Every Side . . .   10

Inaugurating the Sangha's New Monastery at Stone-Screen Cliffs   12

Returning Across the Lake from Our Monastery . . .   13

Dwelling in the Mountains   14

On Stone-Gate Mountain's Highest Peak   56

Overnight at Stone-Gate Cliffs   57

Crossing the Lake from South Mountain to North Mountain   58

Following Axe-Bamboo Stream, I Cross Over a Ridge . . .   59

Stone-House Mountain   60

Final Exile: Nan-hai 431-33

On Lu Mountain   63

Out Onto Master-Flourish Ridge Above . . .   64

In Hsin-an, Setting Out from the River's Mouth at T'ung-lu   65

Beyond the Last Mountains   66

Facing the End   67

Notes   69

Key Terms: An Outline of Hsieh Ling-yün's Conceptual World   75

Finding List   78

Further Reading   79

INTRODUCTION

In ancient China, *mountains* were not merely natural, but sacred objects: they were quite literally sites where the powers of earth met those of heaven. The living universe was made up of *ch'i*, the universal breath, and *yin* and *yang* were the two dynamic aspects of this life force, the fundamental principles whose interaction generates all things in a process of constant transformation. *Yin* and *yang* had many manifestations, such as hot and cold, dark and light, female and male; but their cosmological manifestations were earth and heaven. So mountains were nothing less than the living and breathing forms emerging from the vast interactions of *yin* and *yang* operating on the cosmic scale. Rivers and mountains were together experienced as fundamental manifestations of earth's *ch'i* breathforce: mountains being *yang*, rivers *yin*. And *rivers* themselves formed part of a single cosmic watershed. Beginning in the western mountains where the Star River (our Milky Way) descends to earth, they flow east toward the sea, and there ascend to become again the earth-cradling Star River. Taken together as a single whole, *rivers and mountains* literally means *landscape*, wild landscape as a truly numinous realm.

It was Hsieh Ling-yün (385-433 C.E.) who first forged a poetic world of this numinous realm, thus initiating a tradition of "rivers-and-mountains" (*shan-shui*) poetry that stretches across millennia. Fundamentally different from writing that uses the "natural world" as the stage or materials for human concerns, Hsieh's rivers-and-mountains poetry might best be described as wilderness poetry, poetry that engages or celebrates wilderness of itself and our integral spiritual relationship to it. It invests realistic descriptions of landscape with the philosophy of Taoism and Buddhism, thereby shaping landscape into forms of enlightenment. In so doing, it celebrates a profound and spiritual sense of belonging to the awesome dimensions of wilderness. Indeed, Hsieh's poems chronicle nothing less than the aesthetic and spiritual discovery of wilderness. They read like dispatches reporting back to the human world, where they were in fact very popular, for this was a time of burgeoning interest in landscape and wilderness. And so it is that in Hsieh Ling-yün's poetry begins, at least for literate human cultures, a practice of the wild that has become essential in our own time.

Hsieh's influence is not limited to a particular genre of Chinese poetry, however: wilderness provides the context for virtually all poetic thinking in ancient China. Indeed, Hsieh's practice of the wild became more and more central to all Chinese culture, for wilderness constitutes the very terms of self-cultivation throughout the centuries in China. This is most clearly seen in the arts, which were nothing less than spiritual disciplines: calligraphers, poets, and painters aspired to create with the selfless spontaneity of a natural force, and the elements out of which they crafted their artistic visions were primarily aspects of wilderness: star and moon, river and mountain, field and garden. It can also be seen, for instance, in the way Chinese intellectuals would sip wine as a way of dissolving the separation between self and "natural world," or tea as a way of heightening and clarifying awareness of the "natural world," practices that ideally took place outdoors or in an architectural space that aspired to be a kind of eye-space, its open walls creating an emptiness that contained the world around it. The ideal of living as a recluse among the mountains also inspired the widespread practice of traveling through particularly beautiful natural areas, which generated an extensive travel literature that is often said to have originated with Hsieh Ling-yün. Meditation, which was widely practiced, was also recognized as a fundamental form of belonging to natural process. But Hsieh's importance is not by any means limited to Chinese culture, for the rivers-and-mountain tradition he inaugurated represents the earliest and most extensive literary engagement with wilderness in human history. Hsieh's work feels utterly contemporary, and in an age of global ecological disruption and mass extinction, this engagement with wilderness makes these poems more urgently and universally important by the day.

❖

Although Hsieh was clearly a mountain recluse at heart, he was inextricably tangled by birth in the virulent politics of his time. His was a typically chaotic and violent period of Chinese history. When the Han Dynasty collapsed in 220 C.E., China fell into fragmentation and instability that lasted until the country was again unified under the Sui and T'ang dynasties, over 350 years later. In 317, for the first time in history, "barbarians" took control of the north, the ancient cradle of Chinese civilization, and the Chin Dynasty was forced into the southeast, a colonial region populated primarily by indigenous, non-Chinese people. This Eastern Chin Dynasty established its capital in Chien-k'ang (present-day Nanjing), but imperial authority was weak and heavily dependent on powerful factions of the aristocracy. Fierce struggles for power among these factions led to substantial internal warfare. And to maintain its wealth, the aristocracy reduced much of the peasantry to virtual slavery on the vast tracts of land it had appropriated. This led to a number of popular rebellions in Hsieh's time, involving widespread warfare and destruction. Meanwhile, the government periodically undertook massive military campaigns to reclaim the north, all of which ended in disaster.

Ironically, this was also a time of great achievement and transformation in Chinese culture. Feeling Chinese culture was under seige, members of the aristocracy felt a kind of historical imperative to cultivate their tradition and renew it. Most of their epoch-making accomplishments can be seen as part of a profound new engagement with wilderness that arose for several reasons: the recent immigration of these intellectuals to the southeast, where they were enthralled by a new landscape of serenely beautiful mountains; the perilous political culture, which drove many intellectuals to retire into the mountains rather than risk the traditional career of public service; and recent philosophical developments (discussed below, pp. xii f.), primarily the revival of Taoist organicist thought, the influx of Buddhist thought from India, and the intermingling of these two traditions. The artistic accomplishments of the age were indeed revolutionary. The origins of Chinese landscape (also *shan-shui*) painting can be traced to this time, and calligraphy was transformed by the organic spontaneity of Wang Hsi-chih, often called the greatest of Chinese calligraphers, and his no less great son, Wang Hsien-chih. Developments in the field of poetry were perhaps even more dramatic. Chinese poetry is traditionally divided into two modes, both of which began at this time: "fields-and-gardens," which begins with T'ao Ch'ien (365-427), and Hsieh Ling-yün's "rivers-and-mountains." However reductive this dichotomy may be, it reflects not only Hsieh's importance in the Chinese poetic tradition, but also the importance of wilderness in that tradition, for the two modes are only distinguished by the aspect of wilderness that they emphasize: peopled, on the one hand, and unpeopled on the other.

The Hsieh family was perhaps the most illustrious family in the aristocracy at this time (Hsieh's mother came from the other preeminent family, the Wangs), and it was heavily involved in contemporary political struggles. In fact, the family lost most of its prominent leaders to these conflicts. As a member of this family, Ling-yün was expected to take his proper place in the Confucian order by serving in the government as his illustrious ancestors had done. And indeed, Hsieh entered the government before he was even twenty, spending the next two decades actively engaged in the dangerous infighting between powerful factions.

Hsieh remained true to the prevailing trend among the great families to side with the more culturally refined factions in opposition to the more vulgar ones, for they felt government should represent the beseiged Chinese cultural tradition they were defending and cultivating so assiduously. Nevertheless, the opposition steadily increased its power, and eventually overthrew the Chin Dynasty, replacing it with the Liu-Sung Dynasty. Although he very nearly lost his life in the failure of a rebellion against Liu Yü, the leader of this opposition faction, Hsieh went on to serve under Liu for some years, both before and after Liu usurped the throne. Two years after taking the throne, Liu was sick and dying. This precipitated a power struggle over who his successor would be, and Hsieh was closely allied with one of the two most likely successors, a prince preferred by the great families for his highly cultivated sensibility. Once again Hsieh found himself on the losing side; and in 422, at the age of thirty-seven, he was exiled to Yung-chia on the southeast coast.

During his journey to Yung-chia, Hsieh's intimacy with wild landscapes deepened, a transformation catalyzed by a visit to the family estate in Shih-ning that had been neglected for years and probably suffered extensive damage when overrun during the peasant rebellions. He fell in love with the spectacular alpine setting and arranged for the repair of his estate, apparently with thoughts of returning there to live as a mountain recluse. In Yung-chia, an ailing Hsieh spent the first six months convalescing at his home perched on a mountainside overlooking the seacoast. During this time of quiet study and contemplation in breathtaking surroundings, Hsieh's grief at exile was replaced by the realization that he had violated his true nature for twenty years in a futile and very dangerous struggle for position. Amid the splendor of Yung-chia's seacoast-mountain landscapes, the combination of this realization with Hsieh's long Taoist and Buddhist practice seems to have brought him to a kind of enlightenment that made his unprecedented rivers-and-mountains poetry possible (a process summarized in the first poem of this book). Neglecting his official duties as local governor in order to explore the mountains and shores, Hsieh began to develop the kind of wilderness poem that earned him such a preeminent place in the Chinese tradition.

Hsieh resigned from government service a few months later and returned to live as a recluse at the family estate in the Shih-ning mountains (p. 6). The one honorable alternative to government service for the educated class in Confucian society, such retirement generally reflected a commitment to the spiritual fulfillment of a secluded life, an act of protest against an unworthy government, or some combination of the two. In Hsieh's case, the spiritual impulse was clearly primary, but given his position as the most prominent member of the Hsieh family, his retirement represented a powerful and even risky criticism of the government. Hsieh spent nearly all of his next ten years in the mountains, and his passion for wandering alpine landscapes only increased. Indeed, this passion led him to invent a special cleated hiking shoe. Equipped with these shoes, a knapsack and a broad-brimmed peasant's hat, he would often set out into the mountains and not be seen for days. It was during this period that he wrote most of his major poems, poems that not only established him as one of the most important poets in the Chinese tradition, but also made him the most celebrated poet of his day.

For Chinese intellectuals, living as a recluse did not normally mean living the ascetic life of an isolated hermit. Instead, it meant living a highly cultivated life in a secluded mountain setting, complete with family and visiting friends. Hsieh Ling-yün's work is central in this recluse tradition, especially his extraordinarily long prose-poem (*fu*) entitled "Dwelling in the Mountains" (pp. 14ff.), which describes his recluse life in exhaustive detail. For Hsieh, this life meant a comfortable mountain-side house, which included an enormous library and vast landscape gardens, and a smaller retreat atop Stone-Gate Mountain that could be reached only after a long hike from the main house. And although secluded, Hsieh's estate was hardly isolated. Many of China's great families had their estates in that region, and that alone would have provided a great deal of sophisticated and like-minded companionship. But Hsieh also maintained a monastic center that attracted visiting monks from near and far, including a number of illustrious dharma masters.

Hsieh's recluse life was cut short in 431, when he was exiled a second time because of his simmering antagonism toward the government in power. Hsieh was compelled to leave his Shih-ning mountains for an exile post as local governor far to the southeast, but he refused to begin work there. And when the government tried to arrest him for insubordination, Hsieh organized a small armed rebellion that was senseless and obviously futile— a gesture of opposition as courageous as it was theatrical. Normally this would have meant immediate execution. But Hsieh was not only the patriarch of the empire's most illustrious family, he was also a celebrated calligrapher and the most renowned poet of the age. The emperor was therefore reluctant, perhaps even afraid, to execute him. Instead, Hsieh was banished to Nan-hai on the southern coast. There, beyond the southern fringes of Chinese civilization, his intransigence apparently continued until he was finally executed in 433.

❖

The traditional terms of enlightenment such as Hsieh came to in his Yung-chia exile can be found in the spiritual ecology of Lao Tzu and Chuang Tzu, the originary Taoist sages. We might approach their Way (Tao: see Key Terms, and for a more extensive account of what follows, my *Tao Te Ching*, especially the Introduction pp. x and xvi ff., and sections 1, 2, and 40) by speaking of it at its deep ontological level, where the distinction between being (*yu*) and nonbeing (*wu*) arises. Being can be understood provisionally in a fairly straightforward way as the empirical universe, the ten thousand living and nonliving things in constant transformation; and nonbeing as the generative void from which this ever-changing realm of being perpetually arises. Within this framework, Way can be understood as a kind of generative ontological process through which all things arise and pass away as nonbeing burgeons forth into the great transformation of being. This is simply an ontological description of natural process, and the Taoist sage dwelt as an organic part of that process. In this dwelling, self is but a fleeting form taken on by earth's process of change– born out of it, and returned to it in death. Or more precisely, never *out of it*: totally unborn. Our truest self, being unborn, is all and none of earth's fleeting forms simultaneously.

The numinous rivers-and-mountains realm represents this cosmology of natural process in its most comprehensive and awesome manifestation. Its basic regions appear almost schematically in countless paintings from the Chinese landscape tradition, a tradition especially influenced by Hsieh: the pregnant emptiness of nonbeing; the landscape of being as it burgeons forth in a perpetual process of transformation; and then, nestled within this self-generating and harmonious Cosmos, the human.

There is a profound loneliness in the vistas of these sparsely peopled land-scapes so dramatically burgeoning forth out of vast realms of emptiness, and that loneliness is a constant presence in Hsieh Ling-yün's poetry. For all its tranquil dwelling, it remains always a poetry of exile. Hsieh knew this exile all too immediately in the political exile he endured, but exile goes much deeper than that, for it describes our state of dwelling within the relentless transformation of natural process in which everything is always on its way somewhere else. In death, Hsieh became an emblematic figure of this exile in natural process, for in spite of his stature as a poet both during and after his life, almost none of his work has survived the erosion of history. From a vast corpus containing no less than a hundred *chüan* (sections or books) of poetry and a hundred *chüan* of other writing, only four *chüan* in each category survive.

Hsieh's assiduous spiritual practice focused on meditation, for in meditation you can watch this Taoist cosmology unfold in all its lonely splendor, as thought burgeons forth from emptiness and disappears back into it. And going deeper into meditation, the mind simply dwells in the generative void, which is nothing less than the emptiness that preceded the universe itself. With this meditative dwelling in the emptiness of nonbeing, you are at the heart of Taoist spiritual ecology, inhabiting the primal universe in the most profound way. Here the awesome sense of the sacred in this generative world is perfectly apparent– for each of the ten thousand living and nonliving things, consciousness among them, seems to be miraculously burgeoning forth from a kind of emptiness at its own heart, and at the same time it is always a burgeoning forth from the very heart of the Cosmos itself.

Though the fundamental elements in this Taoist cosmology of natural process remained unchanged, it was being refashioned among intellectuals of Hsieh's time by Buddhist doctrine that had recently migrated from India, a process that eventually produced Ch'an (Zen) Buddhism, the distinctively Chinese form of Buddhism that became so influential in Chinese intellectual culture. During his cosmopolitan years of political involvement, Hsieh came to know the two most prominent Buddhist figures of the time, both of whom were of historic importance in the development of Buddhism in China. The first was Hui Yüan (334-416), who founded the renowned East-Forest Monastery high in the Lu Mountains. There, Hui emphasized *dhyāna* (sitting meditation) as he taught a form of Buddhism that contained early glimmers of Ch'an (*ch'an* is the Chinese translation of *dhyāna*). Although it was a legendary meeting with Hui at his Lu Mountain monastery that originally brought Hsieh to serious Buddhist practice, it was the second of these Buddhist masters who had the most profound impact on Hsieh's thought: Tao-sheng (ca. 360-434).

Tao-sheng was the first in China to advocate the principle of total and instantaneous enlightenment, a fact which has led people to trace the origin of Ch'an to him. While exiled in Yung-chia and beginning to develop his rivers-and-mountains poetics, Hsieh Ling-yün wrote "Regarding the Essence" (*Pien Tsung Lun*), an essay that outlines Tao-sheng's ideas on enlightenment. Generally considered the earlist surviving Ch'an text in China, this work indicates that Hsieh had a profound grasp of Tao-sheng's ideas and confirms that he had probably undergone a kind of Ch'an enlightenment himself. Hsieh dismisses the traditional Buddhist doctrine of gradual enlightenment because "the tranquil mirror, all mystery and shadow, cannot include partial stages":

> one must become nonbeing and mirror the whole, for the
> inner pattern (*li*) is absolute and total.

Taoist cosmology remains little changed in this doctrine: enlightenment means to become the emptiness of nonbeing, and as such mirror being as it unfolds according to the *inner pattern* (see Key Terms: *li*), a key concept that recurs often in Hsieh's poetry. The philosophical meaning of *li*, which originally referred to the veins and markings in a precious piece of jade, is something akin to what we call natural law. It is the system of principles according to which the ten thousand things burgeon forth spontaneously from the generative void, each according to its own inner pattern, independent and self-sufficient, each dying and returning to the process of change, only to reappear in another self-generating form. *Li* therefore weaves nonbeing and being into a single boundless tissue. For Hsieh, one comes to a deep understanding of *li* through *adoration* (see Key Terms: *shang*), another recurring concept in the poems. *Shang* denotes a kind of aesthetic experience of the wild mountain realm as a single overwhelming whole. It is this aesthetic experience that Hsieh's poems try to evoke in the reader, this sense of dwelling that is fundamentally the same as the dwelling described by the early Taoists, for crucial to Hsieh's vision of an undifferentiated whole is a self that is not differentiated from that whole, and is therefore "unborn."

Later writers would describe *li* in the context of *ch'i*: they understood *ch'i* as the material aspect of the universe, and *li* as its inner aspect. But concepts at these depths blur, especially in this intermingling of Taoist and Buddhist thought, and in the hands of various writers *li* appears virtually synonymous with a host of other key concepts: even Way (Tao) itself and *tzu-jan* (see Key Terms), the mechanism or process of Way's unfolding in the empirical world; or Buddha and *prājña*, the Buddhist term for enlightenment in which self is identified with the emptiness that is the true nature of all things.

The meditative identification of mind with nonbeing had been part of Taoist practice from the beginning, and in Hsieh's time the proto-Ch'an Buddhism of Hui-yüan and Tao-sheng was focusing on it more and more (*ch'an* literally means *meditation*). Hsieh diligently practiced such meditation in the mountains, but his poetic practice of the wild was an extension of this meditative identification with nonbeing into the more complete enlightenment he described in his "Regarding the Essence" (which is also a more complete form of loneliness). As with China's great landscape paintings, Hsieh's mountain landscapes enact "nonbeing mirroring the whole," rendering a world that is profoundly spiritual, and at the same time, resolutely realistic in its extensive descriptions.

Here lies the difficulty Hsieh's work presents to a reader. It is an austere poetry, nearly devoid of the human stories and poetic strategies that normally make poems engaging. Hsieh's central personal "story" is the identification of enlightenment with wilderness, and this is precisely why Hsieh has been so admired in China. Rendering the day-to-day adventure of a person inhabiting the universe at great depth, Hsieh's poems tend more to the descriptive and philosophical, locating human consciousness in its primal relation to the cosmos. In so doing, they replace narrow human concerns with a mirror-still mind that sees its truest self in the vast and complex dimensions of mountain wilderness. But as there was no fundamental distinction between mind and heart in ancient China, this was a profound emotional experience as well, and it remains so for us today. With their grandiose language, headlong movement and shifting perspective, Hsieh's poems were especially celebrated for possessing an elemental power that captures the dynamic spirit and inner rhythms that infuse the numinous realm of rivers and mountains; and reading them requires that you participate in his mirror-still dwelling. Hsieh's great poems may seem flat at first, and very much alike– but in that dwelling, each day is another form of enlightenment, and each walk another walk at the very heart of the cosmos itself.

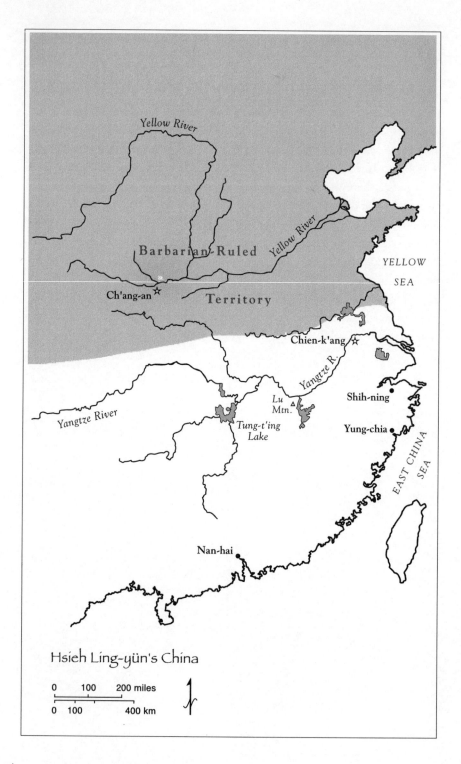

Yellow River

Barbarian-Ruled

Yellow River

Ch'ang-an ☆

Territory

YELLOW
SEA

Chien-k'ang ☆

Yangtze R.

Lu
Mtn. △

Shih-ning

Yangtze River

Tung-t'ing
Lake

Yung-chia •

EAST CHINA
SEA

Nan-hai •

Hsieh Ling-yün's China

0   100   200 miles

0   100   400 km

FIRST EXILE: YUNG-CHIA, 422-23

ON A TOWER BESIDE THE LAKE

Quiet mystery of lone dragons alluring,
calls of migrant geese echoing distances,

I meet sky, unable to soar among clouds,
face a river, all those depths beyond me.

Too simple-minded to perfect Integrity
and too feeble to plow fields in seclusion,

I followed a salary here to the sea's edge
and lay watching forests bare and empty.

That sickbed kept me blind to the seasons,
but opening the house up, I'm suddenly

looking out, listening to surf on a beach
and gazing up into high mountain peaks.

A warm sun is unraveling winter winds,
new *yang* swelling, transforming old *yin*.

Lakeshores newborn into spring grasses
and garden willows become caroling birds:

in them the ancient songs haunt me with
flocks and flocks and *full lush and green*.

Isolate dwelling so easily becomes forever.
It's hard settling the mind this far apart,

but not something ancients alone master:
that serenity is everywhere apparent here.

INSPECTING FARMLANDS, I CLIMB THE BAY'S COIL-ISLE MOUNTAIN

If anything can ease the grief of exile travels
it's these morning winds and seascape vistas,

vast swells stretching away beyond knowing
to the east, that unfathomable Great Valley.

I'll follow the way of water-chestnut foragers,
traces of drifting song thinning sorrow away,

roam along beaches of jade-green sand at ease,
wander these cinnabar-red peaks of eternity.

CLIMBING GREEN-CLIFF MOUNTAIN IN YUNG-CHIA

Taking a little food, a light walking-stick,
I wander up to my home in quiet mystery,

the path along streams winding far away
onto ridgetops, no end to this wonder at

slow waters silent in their frozen beauty
and bamboo glistening at heart with frost,

cascades scattering a confusion of spray
and broad forests crowding distant cliffs.

Thinking it's moonrise I see in the west
and sunset I'm watching blaze in the east,

I hike on until dark, then linger out night
sheltered away in deep expanses of shadow.

Immune to high importance: that's renown.
Walk humbly and it's all promise in beauty,

for in quiet mystery the way runs smooth,
ascending remote heights beyond compare.

Utter tranquillity, the distinction between
yes this and *no that* lost, I embrace primal

unity, thought and silence woven together,
that deep healing where we venture forth.

THE JOURNEY HOME

.   .   .

It's late autumn, heaven's compassion-deep
skies bottomless above a world gone frail.

Geese climbing beyond clouds to soar away,
grasses tattered beneath shrouds of frost,

I leave familiar shores of desolate shadow
and sunlit vistas laced with delicate scents.

Leaves tumble through windblown forests.
The moon's radiance filling mirrored waters,

I sail from Green-Field's meandering isles
to the ease of White-Shore's empty pavilion,

the way treacherous, full of strange forms,
mountains on every side all transformation.

I put ashore to rest there, linger on and on
probing traces flushed clouds leave behind,

then drift a crystal-pure hundred-mile lake,
gazing at lone cliffs thousands of feet high:

they've endured forever here, changeless
through this world all flourish and perish,

.   .   .

MOUNTAIN DWELLING: SHIH-NING, 423-32

I'VE PUT IN GARDENS SOUTH OF THE FIELDS, OPENED UP A STREAM AND PLANTED TREES

Woodcutter and recluse– they inhabit
these mountains for different reasons,

and there are other forms of difference.
You can heal here among these gardens,

sheltered from rank vapors of turmoil,
wilderness clarity calling distant winds.

I *ch'i*-sited my house on a northern hill,
doors opening out onto a southern river,

ended trips to the well with a new stream
and planted hibiscus in terraced banks.

Now there are flocks of trees at my door
and crowds of mountains at my window,

and I wander thin trails down to fields
or gaze into a distance of towering peaks,

wanting little, never wearing myself out.
It's rare luck to make yourself such a life,

though like ancient recluse paths, mine
bring longing for the footsteps of friends:

how could I forget them in this exquisite
adoration kindred spirits alone can share?

THERE ARE TOWERING PEAKS ON EVERY SIDE
OF MY SPIRIT'S TRUE HOME ATOP STONE-GATE
MOUNTAIN'S IMPOSSIBLE CRAGS, WINDING
STREAMS AND ROCKY FALLS, THICK FORESTS
AND TALL BAMBOO

Reaching my hut built of quiet mystery
I sweep clouds away and settle into repose.

There's no one left to climb with me beyond
slippery moss and frail vines to this peak

where autumn winds bluster and breeze
and spring grasses grow lush and green.

You're traveling beyond hope of return
now, no interest in those tender reunions

where fragrant dust frosts jewelled mats
and crystalline wine lavishes golden cups,

so why stand watch on stormy lakeshores
or on lookouts among cinnamon branches?

My thoughts wander Star River distances.
A single shadow alone with forgetfulness,

I swim in a lake down beneath cliff-walls
or gaze up at gibbons haunting treetops,

listen as evening winds buffet mornings
and watch dawn sunlight flare at sunset.

Slant light igniting cliffs never lasts long,
and echoes vanish easily in forest depths:

letting go of sorrow returns us to wisdom,
seeing the inner pattern ends attachment.

O but to set out on the sun's dragon-chariot
and soar– that's solace to nurture my spirit,

for these aren't things people understand:
I need to talk them over with a true sage.

INAUGURATING THE SANGHA'S NEW MONASTERY AT STONE-SCREEN CLIFF

Confused and stumbling inside city walls
though time's three regions are boundless,

life's vagrant pleasures blinding the eye
though insight plumbs beginning and end,

we spend our youth awaiting tomorrow,
then watch twilight ruins of age close in.

Sudden as a lightning storm, this dreamed
sleight-of-hand scatters away in a flash:

even good fortune that never leaves you
can't slow the steady vanishing of a life.

We imagined another Spirit-Vulture Peak,
another Jetavana of temples and gardens,

and now, cascades tumbling free at the hall,
we'll sit gazing into all perfect emptiness,

and sunlit forests gracing these windows,
we'll talk out the inner pattern's mystery.

RETURNING ACROSS THE LAKE FROM OUR MONASTERY AT STONE-SCREEN CLIFF

In the transformations of dusk and dawn, skies
fill rivers and mountains with crystalline light,

crystalline light bringing such effortless joy
a wanderer rests content, all return forgotten.

The sun was rising when I left my valley home,
and daylight faint before I started back, sailing

past forested canyons gathering dusky colors
and twilight mist mingling into flushed cloud,

past lotus and chestnut a lavish luster woven
through reeds and rice-grass toppled together.

Then ashore, I hurry south on overgrown paths,
and settle into my eastern home, enchanted still.

When worry ends, things take themselves lightly,
and when thoughts lull, the inner pattern abides.

I offer this to adepts come refining their lives:
try this old Way of mine, make it search enough.

4

Embracing the seasons of heaven through bright insight,
the impulse turning them, and the inner pattern's solitude,

my grandfather came to this retreat in the dusk of old age,
leaving behind his renown engraved in memorial hymns.

He thought Ch'ü Yüan a fool for drowning himself in exile,
admired Yüeh Yi for leaving his country. And he himself–

choosing the sacred beauty of occurrence appearing of itself,
he made the composure of these mountain peaks his own.

5

Looking up to the example that old sage handed down,
and considering what comes easily to my own nature,

I offered myself to this tranquil repose of dwelling,
and now nurture my lifework in the drift of idleness.

Master Pan's early awakening always humbled me,
and I was shamed by Master Shang's old-age insight,

so with years and sickness both closing in upon me
I devoted myself to simplicity and returned to it all,

left that workaday life for this wisdom of wandering,
for this wilderness of rivers-and-mountains clarity.

6

Here where I live,
lakes on the left, rivers on the right,
you leave islands, follow shores back

to mountains out front, ridges behind.
Looming east and toppling aside west,

they harbor ebb and flow of breath,
arch across and snake beyond, devious

churning and roiling into distances,
clifftop ridgelines hewn flat and true.

7

Nearby in the east are
Risen-Fieldland and Downcast-Lake,
Western-Gorge and Southern-Valley,

Stone-Plowshares and Stone-Rapids,
Forlorn-Millstone and Yellow-Bamboo.

There are waters tumbling a thousand feet in flight
and forests curtained high over countless canyons,

endless streams flowing far away into distant rivers
and cascades branching deeper into nearby creeks.

8

Nearby in the south are
two streams flowing together into a single
meander past three islands, all sincerity

doubled around inside out and outside in,
cleaving and fusing rivers and mountains.

Cliffs and pinnacles topple into flight on the east ridge,
curtained across to the west road, above rock-domed

islands where billows fill forests, and swelling waves
sweep white sand together and send water flowing away.

9

Nearby in the west are
Aspen and Guest Peaks sharing a mountain,
Halcyon and Emperor along a lazy ridgeline,

Stone-House Mountain facing Stone-Screen Cliff
across a gorge carved below Tier and Orphan,

its riverbanks thick bamboo coloring the current green,
reflected cliff-light turning mountain streamwater red.

Here the moon's hidden, darkened by peaks and summits,
and in rising wind, a forest of branches breaks into song.

10

Nearby in the north are
paired Shamaness Lakes linked together
and twin Lucent Streams threading ponds,

Perpetua Cliff split from Mount Athwart,
Compass and Blessing Peaks broken apart.

Embankments stretch on away, wandering along lakeshores,
and streams in flood cascading through gorges swell and surge

toward ponds and lakes that meander beneath towering cliffs.
There, among rocks churning with whitewater, the Way opens.

11

Far off to the east are
Tung-Cypress and Celestial-Terrace,
Stone-Window and Boundless-Peace,

Twin-Leeks and Fourfold-Radiance,
Fivefold-Shrine and Three-Reeds,

ranges and peaks all entered in books of divine marvels.
The rapport in things is tangible in the divine blessings

I wander among there, hiking Stone-Bridge's mossy trail
and beyond through the twisting gnarls of Oaken Gorge.

12

Far off to the south are
peaks like Pine-Needle and Nest-Hen,
Halcyon-Knoll and Brimmed-Stone,

Harrow and Spire Ridges faced together,
Elder and Eye-Loft cleaving summits.

When you go deep, following a winding river to its source,
you're soon bewildered, wandering a place beyond knowing:

cragged peaks towering above stay lost in confusions of mist,
and depths sunken away far below surge and swell in a blur.

13

Far off to the west are

. . .

14

Far off to the north are
a long river flowing ever homeward
and the boundless seas taking it in.

Advent Ridge and sandbars wander away,
island mountains crowding together

below summits towering far and wide, sentinels watching over
waters meandering through depths and winding liquid away.

These wildlands, such wonder unceasing: they spread away into
wind-driven waves all struggle and repose together in the end.

15

It's emptiness to gaze along South Road's . . . . . .
  . . . growing cliffs . . . become plateau . . .

  . . . shorelines you can fathom the deep,
and seeing islands understand the shallow,

but when the water swells and billows full, rocks shelving up vanish,
and when the waves settle back clear again, sunken sand reappears.

Once rising winds start billows swelling,
water's power grows fierce and reckless,

and every year in spring and autumn,
the coming of new moons and full moons

startles waves into seething and churning
terror all surging and foundering deep.

Lightning swells and thunder tumbles,
torrents in flight and scattered cascades

brimming over impossible cliffs and rising into peaks
spread across midstream and gathering such distances,

swirling first in a flash and leaping out through the sky,
then toppling over into depths at last, revealing valleys.

A mere description of this realm was enough to cure a prince of Ch'u,
and meeting the Sea Lord here, even the River Spirit was overwhelmed.

16

And among this, our ancient home
remained: house old and garden new,

elm and hibiscus still intertwined,
foundation and well not yet ruins.

There were paths east and west running true among fields,
and roads wandering away in front and back, meandering

alongside exquisite ponds and overlooking awesome gorges,
hugging canyon walls and snaking around mountain slopes.

Thinking about all the divine marvels gracing our country,
how they aren't so plentiful and wondrous anywhere else,

I restored the twin-peaked roof on our house below cliffs
and built a simple one-beam hut up where streams begin.

The south door of one opens onto distant mountain ranges
and the east window of the other looks across nearby fields,

fields spreading to join ridgetops and fill the fertile valleys,
peaks rising over rivers and lakes, trails winding through.

17

And trails cross fields far and wide
among interlaced banks and dikes,

channels carrying water through
veins in fields and away into canals.

Shu rice abounds, lavish with grace,
keng rice too, fragrance swelling,

the early crop ripe at summer's end,
the late top-heavy in early autumn,

and high ground boasts dry fields:
hemp and wheat, millet and beans.

I bide my time, watching the years
bring sowing and reaping around,

keeping ample stores of grain, enough and more for food and drink.
Why bother with craftsmen and merchants, farmers and shepherds,

why measure life by how many treasures you've made your own?
Abide by the inner pattern and a full stomach is sufficiency enough.

18

Slipping from gardens to fields
and from fields on toward lakes,

I float and drift on and on along
rivers to realms of distant water,

sage pools in mountain streams deepening into recluse dark
and hazy confusions of wild rice clearing away along islands.

Fragrant springwater swells into springtime cascades here,
and chilled waves quicken amid autumn's passing clarity.

Wind churning up lakewater around islands full of orchids,
sunlight pours through pepper trees and on across the road,

and soaring lazily over the mid-stream island, the pavillion
there soaked in its luster, the moon in water is a perfect joy.

Lingering out shadows, mornings infuse things with clarity,
and suffusing the air, fragrant scents settle into evenings

here, where thinking of loved ones lost to me forever now,
I can look forward to the evanescent visits of cloud guests.

20

Many cures in *Essential Medicinals*
flourish among mountains and lakes.

Lords Thunder and Maple identified them,
Doctors Accord and Ease learned their uses:

the three seed-nuts and the six roots,
the five flowers and the nine fruits,

the two asparagus sharing a name but differing in nature
and three wolfsbane differing in form but found together,

water-scented orchids that flourish as autumn fades away,
forest orchids coming into lavish bloom when snows fly,

gnarled cypress that can outlive ten thousand dynasties,
and secretive china-root that's hidden a thousand years,

blossoms a radiant whorl of red petals gracing green stems,
leaves lush and silk-white drooping from purple branches.

They strengthen the spirit and make your life last and last,
dispel phantom demons, drive away malaise and affliction.

21

There are bamboo like
the two arrows with distinct leaves
and the four bitters tasting the same,

water and rock in different valleys
and a medley of both course and fine.

They've stood here forever, majestic heights all easy grace,
all flourishing elegance lavish in isolate whispers of wind:

graced with dew through the bitter dark of passing nights,
they shudder and sway in the clear air on breezy mornings,

pitch branch-tips high in the sweep of azure-deep clouds
and loft their kingfisher-greens out over emerald pools.

. . .

22

There are trees like
pine, cypress, sandlewood and oak,
. . . . . . , *wu-t'ung* and elm,

mulberries, rafterwood, stonethorn
and catalpas, tamarisk and ailanthus.

Ranging from steadfast to yielding
by nature, and from durable to frail,

they follow their own ways, rooted in
land high and low, fertile and barren:

trees you can't reach around keeping mountain peaks hidden,
their tops thousands of feet high parading through emptiness,

trees towering up in stately grandeur across ridgelines above
and spreading thick in shade along mountain streams below.

A tangle of hanging branches all through the long canyons,
they crowd together among rocks, making roads impossible

here, where blossoms reflected in water double their radiance
and *ch'i* wandering among them returns on the wind suffused,

where leek-green pines remain lovely through stark winters,
their fragrance growing lavish to welcome warmer weather:

they can bid farewell to autumn's tumble of scattering leaves
and wait out blossoms of spring still tucked inside their buds.

23

Plants, trees, bamboo– they flourish
here, but moving creatures too abound,

flying, swimming, running, leaping.
You won't find root or source for them,

just glimpse shapes and hear sounds.
Roaming these rivers and mountains

according to the seasons, they follow
the impulse of each their own nature.

24

There are fish like
snake-fish and trout, perch and tench,
red-eye and yellow-gill, dace and carp,

bream, sturgeon, skate, mandarin-fish,
flying-fish, bass, mullet and wax-fish:

a rainbow confusion of colors blurred,
glistening brocade, cloud-fresh schools

nibbling duckweed, frolicking in waves,
drifting among ghost-eye, flowing deep.

Some drumming their gills and leaping through whitewater,
others beating their tails and struggling back beneath swells,

shad and salmon, each in their season, stream up into creeks and shallows,
sunfish and knife-fish follow rapids further, emerge in mountain springs.

25

There are birds like
junglefowl and swan, osprey, snow-goose,
crane and egret, bustard and kingfisher,

grouse and magpie like rich embroidery,
thrush and turkey like tasseled medallions,

ducks in dawn gatherings every morning,
pheasants at mountain bridges in season,

sea birds soaring in defiance of the wind,
and northern birds here fleeing the cold:

when buds open, they'll flock back north,
but frost-fall always sends them south again.

Greetings echo across Star River distances
as companions sleep along rivers and lakes:

if you listen to their crystalline calls here below, you can hear them
carrying Master Wang up through immortality skies and beyond,

and before long they're crossing back, returning on anxious wings
to the lavish pleasures that fill their days in these radiant valleys.

26

On mountaintops live
gibbon, jackel, wildcat and badger,
fox and wolf, cougar and bobcat,

and in mountain valleys
black and brown bear, coyote, tiger,
bighorn and deer, antelope and elk.

Things gambol among branches soaring out over cliffs
and leap across rifts of empty sky within deep gorges,

lurk down through valleys, howls and roars perpetual,
while others climb, calling and wailing among treetops.

27

Hook and line are never cast
here, and nets never spread;

no one shoots strung arrows
or sets out traps and snares.

If you look, the Humanity of wolves and tigers is clear,
but there's no limit to the passion for killing such things.

I devoted myself to Way long ago, when I was still young,
awakening to the love all beings naturally feel for life,

and was led by this to see it throughout the realm of things.
By now, never far from my dwelling place in this love,

I nurture the easy joy of soaring gulls and darting fish,
no hint of *mechanical mind* here among forest and lake.

28

I reverently welcome sage teachings
and humbly study the ancient sutras

here in luminous mountain expanses
far from towns full of meat's stench.

The Great Vow of Limitless Compassion
saving all things from deep confusion—

it's nothing but feckless chatter in places crowded with people.
It needs the nourishment of Way's solitude to fulfill its nobility.

We revere the blooming radiance of Buddha's Deer Park gardens
and admire the summit of his renowned Spirit-Vulture Mountain,

yearn for the pure forests resounding with his voice in Kevaddha
and long for the fragrant gardens where he taught in Amrapali:

but however distant and remote the Buddha's pure face may seem,
they say the sounds of his lament are always with us everywhere,

so I built a monastery among the quiet mystery of high peaks,
hoping monks would come, walking-sticks in hand, and find repose.

These sitting cushions seem gifts given by Pradiparaja Buddha
and our meals perfect kindness offered by Gandhakuta Buddha.

Here, our struggles all fading away, thought sees through it all,
and this close to the inner pattern, antiquity continues refreshed.

29

Plans beginning to form, I set out,
walking-stick in hand, hiking alone

through gorges and across streams,
into mountains and over ridgelines,

crossing summits without resting,
tracing creeks back without pause.

Combed by wind and rinsed by rain,
or stepping into dew among the stars,

I sifted through our shallow thoughts
and left their tight compass behind.

Without shell or stalk for divination,
I picked out the fine and wondrous,

cut thornwood staffs and blazed trails
in my search for boulders and cliffs.

Here, four mountains circled round,
a pair of streams winding through,

I soon had a library
facing south ridges

and a teaching hall
against north slopes,

a hall for meditation
among sheer peaks

and huts for monks
along deep streams.

Looking into these towering forests hundreds of years old,
I inhabit the savory fragrance of ten thousand passing ages,

and turning to the fresh springs of all boundless antiquity,
treasure the inexhaustible clarity of their glistening liquid.

Leaving behind the elegant towers that stand outside cities
and the human enterprise bustling inside every village wall,

I delight here in origin's weave, embrace uncarved simplicity,
heaven and earth mingling sweet dew in these fields of Way.

30

Bitter-season pure, dharma masters
illuminate all they nurture deep:

minds settled beyond appearance
and yet devoted to their students,

they wander among leaning rocks,
rest beneath simple thatched roofs.

In the steady vanishing of seasons
they know the deceit of possession,

and looking across time's three regions, they find only dream.
They embrace the Six Paramitas, cultivating Way through them,

and blending thought and silence into a tranquil anchorage,
they cherish the recluse depths of living the inner pattern.

32

To tend such mountains and waters
takes plenty of managers leading

workers of surpassing devotion
diligent throughout the seasons:

we climb summits and fell trees,
clear thornwood and cut bamboo,

dig shoots from bamboo thickets
and open up broad-leaf in valleys,

more carambola than we can gather,
pokeberry good autumn and winter.

Among blossoming vines, we forage
wild grapes across field and stream,

make wines all mountain clarity
promising bright joy and fortune,

bitter finished clean with thistle,
sweet ripened through with *shen*.

We cut mulberry in towering forests
and peel *chi*-bark on cragged peaks,

dig madder-root below sunlit cliffs,
and pick *hsien* on shaded headlands.

You can see thatch gathered by day
and rope braided through nights,

wild rice scythed and rushes cut
for woven mats and savory meals,

and mud transformed into pottery.
There's no limit to our harvest here,

even burnt ash, and charcoal too.
Everything according to its season

(honey gathered in the sixth month
and grain threshed in the eighth),

we bring in such abounding stores
the calendar is beyond all telling.

33

As for my
homes perched north and south,
inaccessible except across water:

gaze deep into wind and cloud
and you know this realm utterly.

34

At South Mountain,
three parks compassed by ridges
and two fields tight among canals,

nine springs swell into cascades,
five valleys to unearthly summits,

a confusion of ragged peaks towering up on all sides,
their slopes a throng of ascending knolls and shoulders,

and nearby, water floods down into surrounding fields,
following a tight network of dikes that stretches far-off,

far-off dikes connecting footpaths,
nearby streams opening cascades.

Crossing ridges and drifting waves
I go by water and return by foot,

return wandering and go roaming
winding isles and ringed pinnacles:

how could anything compare to this
joy and beauty so perfectly apparent?

I built my hut up here, facing northern summits,
its porch opening out onto vistas of southern peaks,

cliffs cragged up and spread away through the door,
an array of mirrored waves billowing at the window.

Taking cinnabar mist and haze for crimson lintels
and emerald clouds for kingfisher-green roofbeams,

I watch shooting stars streak down across the sky
and turn to gaze .   .   .   .   not yet out herding.

It isn't just swallows and sparrows that flutter short:
even soaring junglefowl and geese never make it

here, where a side spring surges
and tumbles down past the eastern eaves,

and between mighty opposing cliff-walls,
sounds of slipping rock fill the western eaves.

Tall bamboo stand in thick tangles of such delicate grace
and thickets of majestic trees deep in their lush seclusion:

vines spreading and spreading, climbing and wandering,
blossoms everywhere sweet fragrance and enticing beauty,

sun and moon cast their radiance over all these branches,
wind and dew opening utter clarity across forbidding peaks.

Summers cool and winters warm,
I abide by seasons, taking my ease

among winding stairs and terraces,
rafters and beams mounting apart.

My hut *ch'i*-sited among all this,
I delight in water and savor rock,

and watching things close at hand
year in and year out, I never tire,

though it hurts to see such beauty following change away.
Lamenting how we only borrow these drifting years of life,

I left the bustling crowds, vanishing into depths of solitude,
mind perennially given over to this rainbow life of clouds.

35

Feeding small lakes strung
together by coves and bays,

streams gather: the return
ten thousand springs follow.

None alike, they seep or swell,
first surging, then a sheen.

And far-off mountain rivers
trace distances back home.

36

Tracing the way back home here,
I might round North Mountain

on roads built along cliff-walls,
timbers rising in switchbacks,

or I could take the watercourse
way winding and circling back,

level lakes broad and brimming,
crystalline depths clear and deep

beyond shorelines all lone grace
and long islands of lush brocade.

Gazing on and on in reverence
across realms so boundless away,

I come to the twin rivers that flow through together.
Two springs sharing one source,

they follow gorges and canyons
to merge at mountain headlands

and cascade on, scouring sand out and mounding dunes
below peaks that loom over islands swelling into hills,

whitewater carrying cliffs away in a tumble of rocks,
a marshy tangle of fallen trees glistening in the waves.

Following along the south bank that crosses out front,
the snaking north cliff that looms behind, I'm soon

lost in thick forests, the nature of dusk and dawn in full view,
and for bearings, I trust myself to the star-filled night skies.

37

Rivers, mountains, streams, rocks,
islands, shores, wildflowers, trees:

you can attend to the singularity of things like that,
or you can weave them all into their place together:

Here where rivers flow crystal clear, no hint of mud,
and mountains are a blur of forests, never bare stone,

rocks lay strewn along forest edges up to jutting cliffs,
and freshets merge into streams, tumble down valleys

to deep water and meandering islands laced with scents.
Above shores all vagrant sand and bamboo reflection,

wildflowers greet winter with blossoms of frozen color,
and frost-covered trees flaunt their shivering green.

Facing northern shade
I find nestled snow against summer heat,
and facing southern sun
I find gentle warmth against winter cold.

Ridgelines here are
stacked up into systems of recluse summits,
and rising peaks are
crowded close and towering into lofty heights

where floating streams pour into flight, cascading through empty sky
toward swells surging up from the secret depths of mountain caverns.

All these things—
it's their singularity that makes them noble
together, each at ease in its own seasons.

38

Abiding by spring and autumn,
trusting to morning and night,

we plow our own fields for food
and coax mulberries into cloth,

grow vegetables for tender treats
and gather herbs to ease old age.

Elsewhere no concern of mine
I follow my nature without doubts:

I listen to dharma in the morning
and set animals free at nightfall,

savor the inner pattern in books
and render my own mind in song.

Giving voice here to my thoughts,
I trust the steady play of details,

shape them into a weave of words
according to their impulse alone.

39

In North Mountain's two gardens
and South Mountain's three parks,

hundreds of fruit trees in careful
rows spread near and spread far,

orchards laid out in line after line
welcoming dawn and awaiting dusk,

lavishing creek and stream, rising
thick or thin over cliffs and knolls.

Apricot Altar and Mango Garden,
Orange Grove and Chestnut Field

boast all kinds of peach and plum,
pears and dates from far off places,

and reaches of loquat and crabapple
compass valleys and ignite islands,

sweet scents of mulberry-plum drifting among winding peaks
and persimmons draping fruit along shorelines stretching away.

40

Along the dikes between rice-fields
grow sweet-scented rushes in blossom,

smartweed, iris, indigo, shepherd's-purse,
radish and turnip, thyme and ginger.

Green mallow gently tending to the season cradles dew
and white garlic grieved by the times shoulders frost,

while winter leeks spread rippling over shady banks
and spring peas twine and stretch across sunlit shores.

41

Frail and hardly made to last
we crumble away into old age,

touch dry gray hair in grief,
gaze wounded into mirrors.

Hoping for strength against these ruins of age,
I turn to the secrets this temple of clarity offers,

search out rare herbs on mountains of renown.
Crossing spirit-waves, leaving my cart behind,

I set out to pick foxglove on rock-strewn slopes
and gather clear asparagus in bamboo shadow.

I collect wild ginger across serried ridgelines
and brook-iris along streams all quiet mystery,

then search out stalactites in mountain caverns
or dig cinnabar-brights beside crimson springs.

42

Living serene for two seasons
each year, summer and winter,

there are monks from far away,
and all those living nearby too.

Dharma drums sounding clarity
and gatha chants crystalline,

blossoms scatter delicate snows,
and incense wanders air away.

We clarify the shadowy language of boundless kalpas
here, talk out meanings bequeathed in dharma images

and cultivate mind to a mere hairsbreadth and beyond,
perfecting these ten thousand inner patterns of life,

the southern Guide Star revealing our true destinies,
the northern Pivot Star returning us to lucid clarity.

There's such contentment in this, and not mine alone.
All of these noble-minded guests share in it with me:

among mountains all clarity and solitude,
they each drift away and lose themselves,

and sounds heard grown altogether rare,
they rejoice, gazing into the inner pattern.

When winter wind scratches and chafes,
we face south and the enduring warmth,

and when summer's radiance blazes down,
we face north where frost and snow abide.

We pause on ascending terraces as we climb up among cloud-roots
and sit beside cascading streams as we wander beyond wind-caves,

delighting to inhabit high atop these mountain walls
this inexhaustible bequest handed down through all antiquity.

47

In these remote and secluded depths of quiet mystery,
silence boundless, distances empty,

you see endeavor denies our nature
and appearance the inner pattern.

When eyes and ears can tell us nothing of such things,
how could anyone follow the path with mere footsteps?

I've distilled all antiquity in the steady cycle of seasons,
trusting to the enlightened insight of five-fold vision,

and now, abiding by this wisdom, I let my brush rest,
let shallow thoughts settle away and these words end.

ON STONE-GATE MOUNTAIN'S HIGHEST PEAK

I started thinking of impossible cliffs at dawn
and by evening was settled on a mountain-top,

scarcely a peak high enough to face this hut
looking out on mountains veined with streams,

forests stretching away beyond its open gate,
a tumble of talus boulders ending at the stairs.

Mountains crowd around, blocking out roads,
and trails wander bamboo confusions, leaving

guests to stray on clever new paths coming up
or doubt old ways leading people back home.

Hissing cascades murmuring through dusk,
the wail of gibbons howling away the night,

I keep to the inner pattern, deep in meditation,
and nurturing this Way, never wander amiss.

Mind now a twin to stark late autumn trees
while eyes delight in the flowering of spring,

I inhabit the constant and wait out the end,
content to dwell at ease in all change and loss,

in this regret no one here's kindred enough
to climb this ladder of azure clouds with me.

OVERNIGHT AT STONE-GATE CLIFFS

I spent the morning digging out orchids,
afraid frost would soon leave them dead,

passed the night among fringes of cloud,
savoring a moon up beyond all this rock,

chortles telling me birds have settled in,
falling leaves giving away fresh winds.

Sounds weave together in the ear, strange
unearthly echoes all crystalline distance,

though there's no one to share wonders
or the joys in wine's fragrant clarities.

We'll never meet again now. I sit beside
a stream, sun drying my hair for nothing.

CROSSING THE LAKE FROM SOUTH MOUNTAIN
TO NORTH MOUNTAIN

I set out from sunlit shores just after dawn
and stopped among shadowy peaks at dusk,

leaving the boat to gaze at far-off islands.
Pausing to rest high among thriving pines

where the pitched trail enters recluse depths
above ringed dragon-jade isles all ashimmer,

I see treetops tangling away into sky below,
hear rivers above flooding the Great Valley.

Streams branch past rocks and flow away.
Forest paths are grown over, tracks gone.

Isn't this how heaven and earth touch us,
this exquisite burgeoning forth of things:

young bamboo still wrapped in green slips
and new rushes fluttering purple flowers,

seagulls frolicking along springtime shores
and pheasants at play among gentle breezes?

Embracing change, the mind never tires,
and gazing deep, our love for things grows.

I have no regrets this far from humankind.
It's true there are no kindred spirits here,

but wandering alone I feel only adoration,
and without it, who plumbs the inner pattern?

FOLLOWING AXE-BAMBOO STREAM, I CROSS OVER A RIDGE AND HIKE ON ALONG THE RIVER

Though the cry of gibbons means sunrise,
its radiance hasn't touched this valley all

quiet mystery. Clouds gather below cliffs,
and there's still dew glistening on blossoms

when I set out along a wandering stream,
climbing into narrow canyons far and high.

Ignoring my robe to wade through creeks,
I scale cliff-ladders and cross distant ridges

to the river beyond. It snakes and twists,
but I follow it, happy just meandering along

past pepperwort and duckweed drifting deep,
rushes and wild rice in crystalline shallows.

Reaching tiptoe to ladle sips from waterfalls
and picking still unfurled leaves in forests,

I can almost see that lovely mountain spirit
in a robe of fig leaves and sash of wisteria.

Gathering orchids brings no dear friends
and picking hemp-flower no open warmth,

but the heart finds its beauty in adoration,
and you can't talk out such shadowy things:

in the eye's depths you're past worry here,
awakened into things all wandering away.

STONE-HOUSE MOUNTAIN

Searching out other realms all quiet mystery,
I sail in morning clarity out beyond farmlands,

swept along past shallows crowded with orchids,
moss-covered peaks towering vast and majestic.

Here, Stone-House floats above outland forests,
a waterfall tumbling down off the rocky dome,

its empty cascade drifting through millennia
below summits outlasting the shift of dynasties.

Nowhere near village sights and sounds, distant
wind and mist keep even woodland foragers away,

but after longing to climb peaks since childhood,
I'll keep these close through the dusk of old age.

A sacred land long since wrapped in solitude:
it seems to share this mind adoration conjures,

and come to this accord that's empty of all words,
I gather its blossoms, savor thickets in cold bloom.

FINAL EXILE: NAN-HAI, 431-433

ON LU MOUNTAIN

.   .   .

Above jumbled canyons opening suddenly
out and away, level roads all breaking off,

these thronging peaks nestle up together.
People come and go without a trace here,

sun and moon hidden all day and night,
frost and snow falling summer and winter.

.   .   .

scale cliff-walls to gaze into dragon pools
and climb trees to peer into nursery dens.

.   .   .

no imagining mountain visits. And now
I can't get enough, just walk on and on,

and even a single dusk and dawn up here
shows you the way through empty and full.

.   .   .

OUT ONTO MASTER-FLOURISH RIDGE, ABOVE HEMP-SPRING MOUNTAIN'S THIRD VALLEY

The true essence of these southlands is fire:
cinnamon thriving high into cold mountains,

peaks copper mirrored in jade-green streams,
and springs crimson beneath staircase cliffs.

Hermit wanderers once lost themselves here,
and sage recluses living contented solitude:

it's a perilous journey, and beyond knowing,
this road to heaven so free of all cleverness,

and on it atop this crowd of peaks, I ascend
depths that feel like mist and cloud, finding

no sign of a winged master. This immortality
summit of his– it's an empty fish trap now:

maps and records have blurred and vanished,
and the teachings of carved inscriptions too.

I can't fathom that thousand-year-old world
or things a hundred generations to come,

but wandering alone, I linger out thoughts
and savor tumbling streams in moonlight,

exhausting the fullness brimming moments.
And what has this to do with past or present?

IN HSIN-AN, SETTING OUT FROM THE RIVER'S MOUTH AT T'UNG-LU

Cold cutting through thin openwork robes
and not yet time for gifts of winter clothes:

this season always pitches me into depths
all grief-clotted thoughts of ancient times.

I'll never sail on thousand-mile oars again
or think through the hundred generations,

but Master Shang's distant mind my own
now, and old Master Hsu's recluse ways,

I wander these winds boundless and clear,
and the headlong rush of autumn streams.

Rivers and mountains open away through
that alluring luster cloud and sun share,

and when twilight's clarity infuses it all,
I savor a joy things themselves know here.

BEYOND THE LAST MOUNTAINS

It's in my
slow crossing over this vast range
that inner and outer come apart.

No hidden rivers to travel below
and no smooth paths cleared above–

even mountain deer glimpsing these ridges turn toward home,
and at such peaks, migrant geese turn back on hurried wings.

Having hiked up to climb across the lower slopes
and follow mountain paths wandering up and down,

I look back along this road through toppling peaks,
gaze ahead at the climb through impossible cliffs

toward towering peaks hidden in morning cloud.
Soon I hear evening streams tumbling in cascades

below forbidding arrays of rock,
strange forms I struggle across.

It's less like knolls and summits
than citadels and gate towers:

amid colors rich as embroidery
and whites bright as any moon,

vines grow impossible to climb,
moss-covered rock wet and slick,

.   .   .

FACING THE END

Nothing of Kung Sheng's life was handed down,
and Li Yeh's extinction was absolutely complete.

Old Hsi fathomed the inner pattern, Master Huo
the inevitable nature of things– and both paid.

Cypress endures thick and green in cold frost
and mushrooms quickly tatter and fray in wind:

content that death comes always in its season,
I'm happy whether life lasts long or stops short,

though I still regret my resolve for our people
didn't end among those mountain cliffs of home.

Giving mind up without that utter awakening:
this is the fear that haunted me all these years,

and now my lone hope turns to some future life
where friend and foe share that mind together.

NOTES

Unless otherwise noted, ellipses indicate lacunae in the text.

FIRST EXILE: YUNG-CHIA, 422-23 (C.E.)

3   **quiet mystery**: A recurring term rich with the secular spirituality of Taoism, *yu* also connotes "solitude," "secret beauty," and "rich darkness." Ref: 3.1, 5.2 & 15, 10.1, 37.15, 52.12, 55.1, 59.3, 60.1.

    dragons: As benevolent as it is destructive, the Chinese dragon is both feared and revered as the awesome force of life itself. Being the embodiment of *yang*, the dragon animates all things and is in constant transformation. It descends into deep waters in autumn, where it hibernates until spring, when it rises. As the dragon embodies the spirit of change, its awakening is equivalent to the awakening of spring and the return of life to earth.

    Integrity: The *Te* of the *Tao Te Ching*, *Integrity* means integrity to Tao (Way: see Key Terms) in the sense of "abiding by the Way," or "enacting the Way." Hence, it is Tao's manifestation in the world, especially in a sage master of Tao.

    mind: See Key Terms: *hsin*.

4   **Great Valley**: A figure for Tao that recurs in Hsieh's poetry (see p. 58) and is often used in later poetry. It originates in Chapter 12 of *Chuang Tzu*:

> On his way to the Great Valley in the east, DiligentExpanse happened to meet WhirlWind on the shores of the eastern sea.
>
> "Where are you going?" asked WhirlWind.
>
> "To the Great Valley."
>
> "Why?"
>
> "The Great Valley– it's something else. You could pour into it forever without filling it up, and ladle from it forever without emptying it out. So I'm going there to wander free."

6   The final eighteen lines from the surviving portion of this long prose-poem
    (*fu*). An unknown amount of text is missing at the end.
    heaven: See Key Terms: *t'ien.*

MOUNTAIN DWELLING: SHIH-NING, 423-32

9   ***ch'i*-sited:** It was thought that the different features of a landscape deter-
    mine the movement of *ch'i*, which might be described as the universal
    breath, vital energy, or life-giving principle (see Introduction, p. vii). The
    best site for a house would be determined by a diviner who analyzed how the
    local movements of *ch'i* harmonized with the particular characteristics of
    those who will live in the house.
    adoration: See Key Terms: *shang.*

10 **Star River:** the Milky Way.

11 **inner pattern:** See Key Terms: *li.*
    sun's dragon-chariot: In myth, the sun rides across the sky in a chariot
    pulled by six dragons.

12 **Sangha:** community of Buddhist practitioners.
    time's three regions: past, present and future.
    Spirit-Vulture Peak: A favorite retreat of the Buddha's, and according to
    tradition, the place where he handed down several major sutras.
    Jetavana: monastery and park that became another of the Buddha's favorite
    retreats.

13 **Way:** see Key Terms: *tao.*

14 **grandfather:** Hsieh's ancestral estate in Shih-ning was established by his
    renowned great-great uncle Hsieh An. Ling-yün's grandfather was Hsieh
    Hsüan, who returned to this family estate to live in seclusion after an illustri-
    ous career which included leading the Chinese armies to a decisive victory at
    Fei River (383), thereby saving Chinese civilization from being completely
    overrun by the "barbarians" who already controlled the north. Hsieh Hsüan

developed the estate, but it had been neglected from that time until Ling-yün came, a period of thirty-four years. During this time there were several peasant rebellions against the aristocracy, and the Hsieh estate had probably suffered extensive damage as a result.

Ch'ü Yüan: China's first major poet, Ch'ü Yüan (340-278 B.C.E.) wrote a number of the poems in the *Ch'u Tzu (Songs of the South)* anthology. He was unjustly exiled, and in his grief threw himself into a river and drowned.

Yüeh Yi: Like Hsieh Hsüan and Ch'ü Yüan, Yüeh Yi was a national hero who fell out of favor with his sovereign. Once the sovereign had turned against him because of slanders, Yüeh Yi decided to leave the country rather than risk execution.

occurrence appearing of itself: See Key Terms: *tzu-jan*.

15 **idleness:** Etymologically, the character for idleness (*hsien*) connotes "profound serenity and quietness," its pictographic elements rendering a tree standing alone within the gates to a courtyard, or in its alternate form, moonlight shining through an open gate. This idleness is a kind of meditative dwelling in the process of *tzu-jan* (see Key Terms), a state in which daily life becomes the essence of spiritual practice. This concept is central in other major Chinese poets such as T'ao Ch'ien and Po Chü-i.

Master Pan: Pan Szu (c. 1 c. B.C.E. - 1 c. C.E.), a Taoist recluse known for his profound sayings.

Master Shang: a recluse who was finally coaxed into taking office because of his extreme poverty. He served reluctantly and finally left to end his life traveling among China's famous mountains.

25 **Sea Lord . . . River Spirit:** from the beginning of Chapter 17 in *Chuang Tzu*. There, because the Yellow River is running deep and wide with floodwater, the River Spirit is beside himself rejoicing in his grandeur. But upon reaching the sea and meeting the Sea Lord, he realizes his true proportions.

30 The first eleven lines of the poem.

31 *ch'i:* See note to p. 9.

34 **Master Wang:** Legend says this Master Wang was an immortal who soared away on a white crane. Such images are not to be taken literally, as if Hsieh believed such things, only as a way of expressing the ethereal nature of birds.

36 **Humanity:** Humanity (*jen*) is the touchstone of Confucian virtue. Simply stated, it means to act with a selfless and reverent concern for the well-being of others. (See my translation of *The Analects*, pp. xxxiv and 247.) Here, Hsieh recognizes and values the coherent social organization of such animals, and so denies any privileged position for the human.
mechanical mind: From Chapter 12 of *Chuang Tzu*, where it is suggested that a gardener get an irrigation machine rather than wear himself out carrying water to his fields. The gardener replies:

> "I once heard my teacher say that if you have clever machines, you have mechanical aims; and if you have mechanical aims, you have a mechanical mind. Nurturing a mechanical mind leaves pure simplicity broken. Once that's broken, your divine nature isn't rooted; and if your divine nature isn't rooted, Way no longer carries you along. I know all about your clever machines, and I'd be ashamed to use one."

37 **Great Vow of Limitless Compassion:** a bodhisattva's vow not to leave the world and enter *nirvana*, but to continue working to bring all sentient beings into the liberation of enlightenment.
Deer Park . . . Spirit-Vulture . . . Kevaddha . . . Amrapali: sites in India that were important in Buddha's life. Cf. p. 12
Pradiparaja Buddha . . . Gandhakuta Buddha: incarnations of Buddha who perform inconceivable miracles in the *Vimalakirti Sutra*, chapters 6 and 10 respectively.

39 **uncarved simplicity:** This concept (*p'u*), which is developed in the *Tao Te Ching* (this passage directly echoing section 19), refers to an uncarved block of wood, taken as an analogy for the undifferentiated state of Tao: nonbeing before it emerges into its particular forms in the realm of being.

40 **Six Paramitas:** ideals that guide Buddhist practice: giving, morality, forbearance, zeal, meditation, and *prājñā* (see Key Terms p.76).

49 **set animals free:** In their reverence for the sanctity of life, Buddhists would go to the markets, buy captured animals, and set them free.

53 **gatha:** a Buddhist poem or chant.
kalpa: A cosmic cycle extending from the creation of a world system to its destruction– traditionally given as 4,320,000 years.

55 **five-fold vision:** reflecting the five levels of enlightenment.

58 **Great Valley:** See note to page 4.

FINAL EXILE: NAN-HAI, 431-33

63 This poem survives only as three fragments, the arrangement of which is unknown.
Lu Mountain: Lu Mountain (literally "Thatch-Hut Mountain" or "Hermitage Mountain") was home to the East-Forest Monastery of Hui Yüan, who influenced Hsieh so deeply earlier in his life (see Introduction p. xiii). It became a major monastic center and the locus of a substantial literature, attracting many reclusive intellectuals.
dragon: See note to p. 3.

64 **Master-Flourish Ridge:** A favorite haunt of immortals in legend, Hua-tzu Ridge was named after an ancient recluse immortal named Hua-tzu Ch'i who once soared up and alighted on the summit (hence the "winged master" in line 11).
fish trap: from the end of Chapter 26 in *Chuang Tzu*:

>   The point of a fish trap is the fish: once you've got the fish, you can forget the trap. The point of a rabbit snare is the rabbit: once you've got the rabbit, you can forget the snare. And the point of a word is the idea: once you've got the idea, you can forget the word.
>   How can I find someone who's forgotten words, so we can have a few words together?

65 **Master Shang:** See note to p. 15.

Master Hsü: Hsü Hsün (320-365), a recluse poet and influential immediate predecessor to Hsieh Ling-yün.

66 This is the surviving fragment of a prose-poem (*fu*) written as Hsieh Ling-yün traveled over the last range of high mountains on his journey into exile at Nan-hai on the south coast. From here, it would have felt to Hsieh as if he were leaving forever the civilized world of his homeland, for not only was the southern climate considered malarial and deadly, the region was populated by tribal people who did not speak Chinese.

67 **Kung Sheng . . . Li Yeh . . . Old Hsi . . . Master Huo:** Like Hsieh Ling-yün, these four men all lost their lives for resisting rulers who had usurped power.
mind: See Key Terms: *hsin*.

KEY TERMS
An Outline of Hsieh Ling-yün's Conceptual World

Tao **道** Way

As the generative ontological process through which all things arise and pass away, Tao can be divided into being (the ten thousand living and non-living things of the empirical world in constant transformation) and nonbeing, the generative source of being and its transformations. The Taoist way is to dwell as a part of this natural process. In that dwelling, self is but a fleeting form taken on by earth's process of change. Or more absolutely, it is all and none of earth's fleeting forms simultaneously. See also: Introduction p. xii, and my *Tao Te Ching* pp. x and xvi ff.

   Ref: 13.16, 20.9, 36.7, 39.8, 40.10, 56.14.

Tzu-jan **自然** Occurrence appearing of itself

Tzu-jan's literal meaning is "self-so" or "the of-itself," which as a philosophical concept becomes "being such of itself," hence "spontaneous" or "natural." But a more revealing translation of *tzu-jan* might be "occurrence appearing of itself," for it is meant to describe the ten thousand things burgeoning forth spontaneously from the generative source, each according to its own nature, independent and self-sufficient, each dying and returning to the process of change, only to reappear in another self-generating form. Hence, *tzu-jan* might be described as the mechanism or process of Tao in the empirical world. See also my *Tao Te Ching* pp. xx ff. and 95.

   Ref: 12.

Li **理** Inner Pattern

The philosophical meaning of *li*, which originally referred to the veins and markings in a precious piece of jade, is something akin to what we call natural law. It is the system of principles which governs the unfolding of *tzu-jan*. *Li* therefore weaves nonbeing and being into a single boundless tissue, and to dwell in *li* was a kind of enlightenment for Hsieh. Elsewhere, we find *li* appearing virtually synonymous with a host of other key concepts: even Tao or *tzu-jan*, and Buddha or *prājñā* (consciousness emptied of all contents; or enlightenment in which self is identified with the emptiness that is the true nature of all things). See also: Introduction p. xiii-xiv.

>Ref: 11.2, 12.16, 13.14, 14.2, 27.16, 37.20, 40.12, 49.11, 53.12
>& 20, 55.4, 56.13, 58.22, 67.3.

Shang 賞 Adoration

This recurring term normally refers to aesthetic appreciation or delight, but in Hsieh Ling-yün it is associated with the central philosophical concept of *li*, and so takes on much larger spiritual or philosophical dimensions. For Hsieh, we come to the enlightenment of *li* through *shang*, a kind of rapturous aesthetic experience of the wild mountain realm as a single ecological whole: the overwhelming manifestation engendered by the interplay of being and non-being, heaven and earth, *yin* and *yang*. It is this wondrous experience that Hsieh's poems try to evoke in the reader. See also: Introduction, pp. vii and xiv.

>Ref: 9.20, 58.21, 59.19, 60.14.

Hsin 心 Mind

In ancient China, there was no fundamental distinction between heart and mind: the term *hsin* connotes all that we think of in the two concepts together. In Hsieh Ling-yün this range of meaning often blends into the technical use of *hsin* in Taoism and proto-Ch'an Buddhism, where it means consciousness emptied of all content, or perhaps consciousness as empty awareness. But for Hsieh, who made little distinction between Taoism and Buddhism at this fundamental level, it also partakes of nonbeing, the void from which all things are engendered. See also: Introduction pp. xii-xiv.

>Ref: 3.20, 36.12, 40.3, 45.24, 49.12, 53.11, 56.15, 58.17, 60.14,
>65.7, 67.11 & 14.

T'ien 天 Heaven

From its primitive meaning of "sky," *heaven* became a kind of all-controlling diety in early Chinese culture. Although it always retains connotations of "sky," the early Taoist masters adapted this concept to mean "natural process," the constant unfolding of things in the process of *tzu-jan*, thereby giving it a sacred dimension. For a somewhat different perspective, consider the recurring entity "heaven and earth," which might be conceived as "creative force and created objects." See also: my *Tao Te Ching* pp. xiv, xix-xx, 96.

Ref: 6.1, 14.1, 39.8, 58.11, 64.8.

FINDING LIST

Texts

1. *Hsieh Ling-yün Chi Chiao Chu.* Ku Shao-po, ed. 1986. (Page number).
2. *Hsieh K'ang-lo Shih Chu.* Huang Chieh, ed. 1924. (Chüan and page number).
3. *The Murmuring Stream.* J.D. Frodsham. (Page number in volume one).
4. *Ch'üan Sung Wen* in *Ch'üan Shang Ku San Tai Ch'in Han San Kuo Liu Ch'ao Wen.* Yen K'o-chün, ed. 1894. (*Chüan* and page number).

Page	1. Hsieh Ling-yün Chi Chiao Chu	2. Hsieh K'ang-lo Shih Chi	3. The Murmuring Stream	4. Ch'üan Sung Wen
3	63	2.12a	121	
4	88	2.18b	125	
5	56	2.22b	129	
6	304		40	30.2b
9	114	3.3b	135	
10	174	3.4b	136	
12	110	3.6a	137	
13	112	3.7a	138	
14	318	Sung Shu 67.7a		31.1a
56	178	3.14a	144	
57	183	3.14b	145	
58	118	3.15a	146	
59	121	3.17a	147	
60	72	3.18a	148	
63	194	4.4b	177	
64	196	4.5b	155	
65	47	4.7a	156	
66	371		77	30.1b
67	204	4.21b	78	

FURTHER READING

Chang, Kang-i Sun. *Six Dynasties Poetry*. Princeton: Princeton University Press, 1986.

Chuang Tzu. *Chuang Tzu: The Inner Chapters*. David Hinton, trans. Washington, D.C.: Counterpoint Press, 1997.

Frodsham, J.D. *The Murmuring Stream: The Life and Works of the Chinese Nature Poet Hsieh Ling-yün*. 2 vol. Kuala Lampur: University of Malaya Press, 1967.

———. "The Origins of Chinese Nature Poetry," Asia Major, 8.1 (1960), 68-104.

Lao Tzu. *Tao Te Ching*. David Hinton, trans. Washington, D.C.: Counterpoint Press, 2000.

Mather, Richard. "The Landscape Buddhism of the Fifth Century Poet Hsieh Ling-yün," *The Journal of Asian Studies*, 18 (1958-59), 67-79.

Neinhauser, William. *The Indiana Companion to Traditional Chinese Literature*. Bloomington: Indiana University Press, 1986.

T'ao, Ch'ien. *The Selected Poems of T'ao Ch'ien*. David Hinton, trans. Port Townsend: Copper Canyon Press, 1993.

Westbrook, Francis. "Landscape Description in the Lyric Poetry and 'Fuh on Dwelling in the Mountains' of Shieh Ling-yunn." Unpublished Ph.D. dissertation, Yale University, 1973.